D1518580

Why Do Ships Float?

by Susan Markowitz Meredith

**Science and Curriculum Consultant: Debra Voege, M.A.,
Science Curriculum Resource Teacher**

CHELSEA
CLUBHOUSE
An Imprint of Chelsea House Publishers

Science in the Real World: Why Do Ships Float?

Chelsea Clubhouse
An imprint of Chelsea House Publishers
132 West 31st Street
New York NY 10001

Library of Congress Cataloging-in-Publication Data
Meredith, Susan Markowitz.
        Why do ships float? / by Susan Markowitz Meredith;
        science and curriculum consultant, Debra Voege.
            p. cm. — (Science in the real world)
        Includes index.
    ISBN 978-1-60413-466-7
    1. Floating bodies—Juvenile literature. 2. Archimedes' principle—Juvenile literature.
    3. Ships—Juvenile literature. I. Title. II. Series.

    QC147.5.M47 2010
    532'.25—dc22

                                                    2009004580

Chelsea Clubhouse books are available at special discounts when purchased in bulk quantities for businesses, associations, institutions, or sales promotions. Please call our Special Sales Department in New York at (212) 967-8800 or (800) 322-8755.

You can find Chelsea Clubhouse on the World Wide Web at http://www.chelseahouse.com

Developed for Chelsea House by RJF Publishing LLC (www.RJFpublishing.com)
Text and cover design by Tammy West/Westgraphix LLC
Illustrations by Spectrum Creative Inc.
Photo research by Edward A. Thomas
Index by Nila Glikin

Photo Credits: 5, 12, 14, 15, 17, 21, 22: Alamy; 7, 23: agefotostock; 9: © Edward A. Thomas; 24: U. S. Marine Corps photo by Cpl. Aaron J. Rock; 29: U.S. Navy.

Printed and bound in the United States of America

Bang RJF 10 9 8 7 6 5 4 3 2 1

This book is printed on acid-free paper.

All links and Web addresses were checked and verified to be correct at the time of publication. Because of the dynamic nature of the Web, some addresses and links may have changed since publication and may no longer be valid.

Table of Contents

Words that are defined in the Glossary are in **bold** type
the first time they appear in the text.

Sinking and Floating

Step into a full bathtub. You'll learn a lot about water. As your body sinks into the tub, the water moves out of the way. All around you, it rises.

Now put a metal fork into the tub. It also pushes water away as it settles. But the amount is tiny. Still, you and the fork **displace** water for the same reason. Your weight pulls you down. The force of **gravity** is doing it. Gravity pulls everything down on land, too.

But there is more to the story. Water pushes up on objects that enter it. This upward force is called **buoyancy**.

Opposite Forces

Buoyancy and gravity, then, work in opposite ways. Sometimes gravity pulls an object down more than the water pushes it up. The fork is a good example. It sinks to the bottom of the tub. But sometimes water pushes an object up more than gravity pulls it down. This happens to many objects—even large **ships**.

But how can a huge and very heavy steel ship float when a metal fork sinks? Their shapes are a big part of the answer.

Even very large ships like this one are able to float.

The Shape of Things

Why does shape matter when it comes to floating and sinking? To better understand, follow this thought experiment. First, picture a block of modeling clay on the table in front of you. Now pull off two small pieces that are the same size and weight and roll them into balls.

Place one ball into a pail of water. You'll notice that it sinks quickly. Gravity is pulling it down more than buoyancy is pushing it up.

A ball of clay will sink. But clay weighing the same amount that is shaped into a boat will float.

Next, flatten the other ball of clay and form it into a boat. Now place the boat in the pail. Notice that its bottom settles in the water, but the boat as a whole stays afloat. The water's buoyancy is pushing the boat up more than gravity is pulling it down.

This boy enjoys watching his model sailboat float on a pond.

Shape Made the Difference

Remember that the two pieces of clay weigh the same amount. They act very differently in the water, though. The reason? Their shapes are different. When it comes to water, an object's shape means a lot.

DID YOU KNOW ?

Model Ships Put to the Test

People of all ages enjoy building model boats as a hobby. But not all models are made for fun. Some have a job to do. Testers place these special models in a long tank filled with water. It's known as a towing tank. There, testers observe how each model acts and moves in the water. For builders of ships—the largest of boats—this information is a big help. It tells them how a full-size ship with the same shape will perform at sea.

How Weight Fits In

Look closely at the shapes of the little boat and ball. The clay of the boat is spread out. The boat also has a hollow shape that allows air inside. On the other hand, the ball's clay is packed into a small space.

Although both objects weigh the same amount, their weight is packed differently. This difference is called **density**.

The tighter an object's weight is packed, the greater is its density. The ball's density, then, is greater than the boat's density because the ball's weight is packed into a smaller space.

Density at Home

A walk around the house reveals many objects with different densities. In the kitchen you'll find several examples.

Start with an average-size potato. Weigh it on a scale. Afterward, place a slice of bread on the same scale. Keep adding more slices until their weight equals the potato's weight. Now compare the sizes of the bread and the potato. You'll see that the potato is much smaller than the stack of bread slices—even though they weigh the same amount. The potato, then, is denser than the bread. Its weight is packed into a smaller space.

A potato is denser than bread. This one is much smaller than a stack of bread that weighs the same amount.

If you compare an apple to leaves of lettuce, you'll find that the apple is much denser.

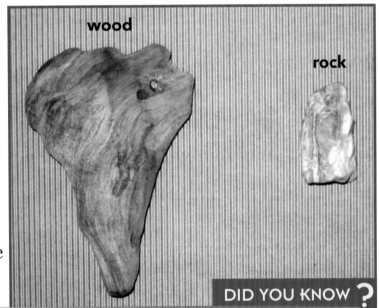

wood

rock

Checking Densities Outdoors

In the yard or the park or the countryside, there are more examples of objects with different densities. For example, let's say you found a rock and a piece of wood that weigh the same amount. Looking at them, you would quickly notice that the wood needs to be much bigger than the rock to match its weight. The wood, then, is less dense than the rock. Interestingly, the wood floats in water, while the rock sinks.

Water Has Density, Too

Just like all things, water has its own density. But what does water's density have to do with clay?

Well, think about the clay ball. All of its weight presses down on the water from one small place. In return, the water pushes back. But it can't push with enough force to keep the dense ball afloat. The ball, then, is denser than the water. So it sinks. In this case, the force of gravity is greater than the water's buoyancy.

The boat is another story. Its weight also presses down on the water. But the weight is spread out more. There is room for air inside the boat, too. Together, the boat's clay and air don't press hard enough in any one place to overcome the water's ability to push back up. The boat, then, is less dense than the water. That's why the boat floats. In this case, the water's buoyancy is greater than the force of gravity.

Changing a Boat's Density

But let's take the experiment one more step. Let's say you go to the

block of modeling clay again and pull off some very small pieces. One at a time, you place pieces of clay in the floating boat. You'll see that with each added piece the boat settles lower in the water. At some point the boat will hold so much extra weight that it sinks. The reason? The boat becomes denser than the water.

The empty boat floats easily. Add the weight of a few balls of clay, and the boat sits lower in the water. Add the weight of enough clay balls, and the boat sinks.

Not All Water Is the Same

Did you know that the density of water changes at different temperatures? The colder the water, the denser it becomes. Also, seawater (saltwater) is denser than fresh water.

Designing a Ship

Designing a ship is not an easy task. These large, heavy boats have to do many things. Most important, they must stay afloat. But they must also travel long distances. Often that means moving across rough seas.

Designers also need to know why the ship is being built. In other words, what is its job? Some ships transport dry cargo like grain and

This large tanker can carry huge amounts of oil.

ore. Some cargo ships, called tankers, carry oil. Other ships are built for passengers only. Still others are used by the military for its missions. There are special ships, too, like icebreakers and research **vessels**.

Because they have different jobs, ships are laid out in various ways. A cruise ship, for instance, looks like a floating city. There is space for restaurants, pools, and shops. There also are floors (or decks) with hundreds of hotel-like rooms. Cargo ships, though, may have just a few giant rooms. A warship may be laid out still differently. Much of its space may be built to carry weapons.

The Same in Some Ways

Whatever their job, all ships are alike in many ways. For one, every ship has a large main body that floats. It also has a power source to drive the ship through water. In addition, every ship is steered in the same way.

DID YOU KNOW ?

Ship Safety

Ships are made to be safe. That's why they all have fire equipment onboard. Lifeboats and life jackets are stored on every ship, too. In case of emergency, every passenger can escape.

A Ship's Hull

A ship's main body is called the **hull**. It is often made of steel or another strong metal. At its base, or bottom, is a long sturdy beam, called a **keel**. The keel goes from the front to the back of the hull. Large steel ribs are attached to the keel, giving the hull its shape. Then big steel plates are placed over the ribs.

The hull is very heavy. But its weight is spread out. Also, there's plenty of room inside for air. So the hull is less dense than the water.

That's why the hull stays afloat. It also floats because it displaces a huge amount of water, whose buoyancy pushes up on the ship.

The hull must move through the water smoothly. That's why the front of the hull, or **bow**, needs the right shape. Many bows are pointed because that shape cuts easily through the water.

The back of the hull, or **stern**, is usually

A ship's bow (or front) is pointed. Its stern (or back) is rounded. The main body of a ship is called the hull. Above the hull is the superstructure.

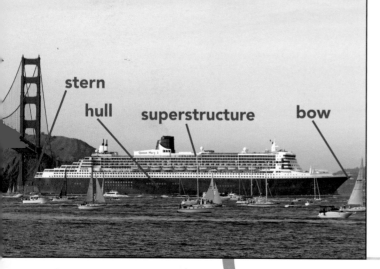

stern

hull   superstructure   bow

rounded. This shape allows the passing water to come together, or close, behind the stern very smoothly.

Keeping a Ship Watertight

Ships have many decks, or levels. The main deck is at the top of the hull. Anything built above the main deck is called the **superstructure**.

Inside the hull, there are special walls called **bulkheads**. They divide the hull into **compartments**. When a compartment's heavy door is shut, that area becomes watertight. If a hull is accidentally torn open in one place, the flooding will likely stay inside one or only a few compartments. The rest of the ship keeps dry. The hull will settle lower in the water. The reason? The hull is now heavier (and denser) because of the weight of the water inside it. Even so, the ship generally can stay afloat.

DID YOU KNOW ?

Why the *Titanic* Sank

Did you know that the *Titanic* (above) had 16 compartments in its hull? Five of them were flooded when the famous ship struck an iceberg in 1912. So much water got into the hull that the ship sank.

Keeping a Ship Steady

A good hull keeps a ship steady as it moves through water. The steadier the hull, the less it rocks from front to back. The less it rolls from side to side, too.

But large ships on rough seas need more than a good hull. They need **stabilizers**. These fin-like surfaces are placed underwater on each side of the hull. They keep the ship from rolling too much. If a ship rolls to the right, for example, the right fin swivels. Its new angle forces more water to flow under it. This extra

Stabilizers keep a ship from rolling from side to side too much in rough water.

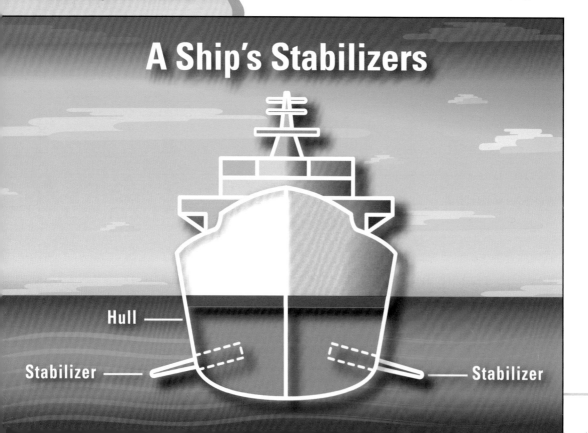

A Ship's Stabilizers

Hull

Stabilizer

Stabilizer

water pushes up on the fin. When the fin moves up, so does the ship. This stops the rightward roll.

Using Ballast

Many ships also stay steady because weight is added to the hull. This weight is called **ballast**. Ships usually use water as ballast. The water is pumped into tanks inside the hull when needed. Empty cargo ships, for instance, need the added weight for stability. When the ship is loaded with goods, ballast water is pumped out.

This ship is pumping out ballast water that it no longer needs.

DID YOU KNOW ?

What Happens to the Water?

Ballast water is very useful for ships. But it can cause problems, too. Water pumped into the ship at a port may have plant or animal **species** living in it. When the ship arrives at another port and dumps ballast water, those species are unloaded, too. But they can harm the native species already living there. One example of an animal that can cause problems if brought to a new area is the spiny water flea. This tiny animal breeds quickly, and it eats the same food that many young fish eat. When the spiny water flea enters a new area, if the native fish cannot get enough food, they die. To help solve this kind of problem, some nations ask ships to follow certain rules when pumping ballast water.

A Ship's Power Source

Today's ships need powerful engines to drive them through the water. Different types of engines have been in use since the early 19th century. But whatever the engine, its main job is to turn a ship's **propeller**. The bigger the ship, the more propellers it has. Small ships have one propeller. The largest ships have four.

Most propellers have several wide blades. They are bolted to the end of a pole, or shaft. The whole unit

Propeller blades are curved. This shape helps move the ship forward.

Why Propeller Blades Are Curved

Fast-moving water has lower pressure

Curved Blade

Propeller

Slower-moving water has higher pressure

Lower pressure pulls the propeller, and the boat, forward

sticks out underwater near the stern. As the propeller turns, each blade pushes the water toward the stern. But the moving water also presses back on the blades. This action pushes the blades—and the ship—forward.

Why Curved Blades Help

Each propeller blade has one curved surface. This also helps move the propeller and the ship forward. How? Follow the path of two drops of moving water. When they meet the propeller blade, they are side by side. One water drop travels over the blade's curved surface. The other drop goes across the blade's other, flatter surface. The water drops reunite at the far end of the blade.

Because the first drop has farther to go (over the curve), it moves faster to meet the other drop at the same time. When water speeds up, its **pressure** gets lower. This low pressure pulls on each propeller blade. The propeller and ship are pulled forward.

DID YOU KNOW ?

Paddle Wheels

Before propellers were invented in 1836, many ships used paddle wheels. One wheel was placed on each side of the ship. As the wheels turned, the vessel moved forward through the water. Steam engines drove these large paddle wheels.

Steering a Ship

A ship may travel fast, but it needs to be steered in the right direction. The ship's **rudder** does that job. Hinged to the stern, this flap swings left and right like a door. The ship's steering wheel, or **helm**, controls the rudder. If the wheel is turned to the right, for instance, the rudder swings right. Its new position is now in the path of fast-moving water. When the water slams into it, the rudder is pushed to the left. This action

By using the wheel to move the ship's rudder, someone steering can turn the ship to the left or the right.

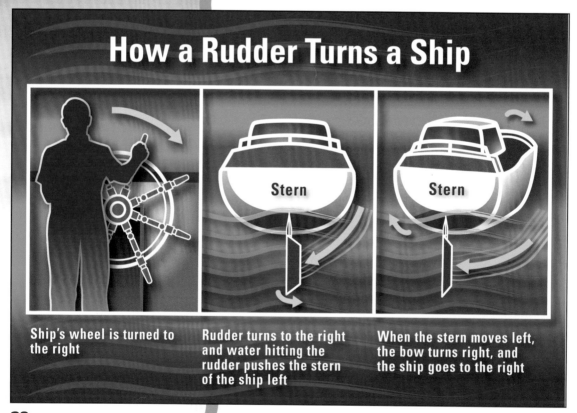

How a Rudder Turns a Ship

Stern

Stern

Ship's wheel is turned to the right

Rudder turns to the right and water hitting the rudder pushes the stern of the ship left

When the stern moves left, the bow turns right, and the ship goes to the right

pushes the stern left, too. The bow then moves to the right. That's the same way the steering wheel was turned!

This bow thruster, in a tunnel in the hull, is used to help steer the ship.

Turning at Slow Speeds

Another device helps steer a ship, too. It's called a **bow thruster**. This small propeller is inside a tunnel in the hull, near the bow. By swiveling, the propeller blades force water to move to the left or right side of the ship. The ship's bow then goes the opposite way. Slow-moving ships coming into port often use their bow thrusters to steer.

DID YOU KNOW ?

Knowing Where to Go

In the middle of the ocean there are no landmarks. So how does the ship's **navigator** know where to go? One way is to observe the sun, moon, and stars. Where are they in the sky? In what direction are they moving? Sailors have been using this method for thousands of years.

Navigation devices like compasses have been around for centuries, too. But today, there are many other useful devices. Modern ships use electronic navigation equipment. Many ships also use GPS, which stands for Global Positioning System, to locate their exact position. This system involves satellites orbiting Earth. A ship can figure out its location by receiving radio signals from several satellites at once.

Ships Doing Business

Every day, thousands of ships carry people and goods to all parts of the world. Even the heaviest cargo ships move safely from port to port. How these ships are loaded is a big part of the reason.

Today, cargo ships have their own "load lines." These marks are painted on the side of the hull. Each mark stands for a different type of water. The highest mark is TF. It means *tropical fresh* water. The lowest is W, which means *winter*. Ships are loaded by the type of water they're in at the time.

Picture an empty ship at a cold North Atlantic Ocean port in January. As cargo is added, the ship settles lower in the water. When the hull

This ship carries many large containers filled with cargo.

sinks to where its W mark touches the water, no more cargo is added.

The Water Line Changes

If the ship stays in cold seawater, the water line stays the same. (The water line is the place on the hull that the surface of the water reaches.) But when the ship enters tropical seas, it settles lower in the water. That's because warm seawater is less dense than cold seawater. Warm seas are less buoyant, too. They don't push up on the ship as much.

Even if the ship moved into fresh water, it would be safe. The reason? With the "load line" system, ships are never overloaded.

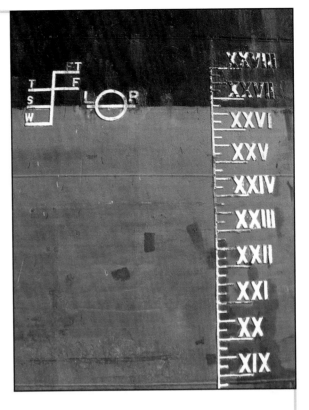

The load lines on this ship are shown in the upper left. W, S, and T on the left side are the lines for winter, summer, and tropical seawater. F and T on the right side are for fresh water and tropical fresh water. (The Roman numeral marks measure the depth of water displaced by the ship.)

"The Sailors' Friend"

Load lines also are called Plimsoll marks. They're named after Samuel Plimsoll, who lived in Great Britain in the 1800s. At that time, it was common for companies to overload ships with cargo. This caused many accidents at sea. To protect sailors, Plimsoll helped pass a law in Parliament. It was known as the Merchant Shipping Act. From then on, British ships had to have load lines on their hulls.

Military Ships

The ships in the U.S. Navy have many jobs to do. An aircraft carrier, for instance, is like a floating airport. Some large carriers can hold up to 95 planes. Carriers have a large flat main deck that the planes use to take off and to land. It is like an airport runway.

Another type of carrier holds troops, weapons, and small landing craft. It is called an **amphibious** warfare ship. It has built-in "docking wells" for the small craft. These wells are closed off from the rest of the ship. They are at the water line. When the small craft are ready to leave—perhaps to carry troops or tanks to shore—the wells are opened. Water rushes in. Once the wells are full, the landing craft float

A small craft enters the docking well of an amphibious warfare ship.

out. Then the small vessels head for land.

Protecting Carriers

Both of these types of carriers do important work. But neither can defend itself from attack. That's why they rely on combat ships like destroyers that travel with them. A destroyer carries weapons for firing on enemy ships and aircraft. It can also hit targets on land. Destroyers can travel through the water at top speeds of more than 30 **knots**. They can move more than twice as fast as oil tankers usually travel.

How Fast Ships Can Go	
Destroyer	33 knots
Aircraft carrier	30 knots
Cruise ship	25 knots
Amphibious warfare ship	20 knots
Supertanker (oil tanker)	15 knots

How Fast Is a Knot?

Did you know that a ship's speed is measured in knots? One knot equals 1 nautical mile per hour. That equals 1.15 miles per hour (1.85 kilometers per hour). Sailors have been measuring speed in knots for a long time. It started in the days when sailing ships were popular. The crew took a long rope and tied knots in it about every 47 feet. Then they wound the rope on a spool. The rope's end dangled in the water. A piece of wood was tied to it. As the ship moved, the spool unwound. Sailors counted how many knots went by in a certain amount of time in order to judge the ship's speed.

Submarines

Submarines are well-designed for traveling underwater. A sub has two hulls, one inside the other. The outer hull is the right shape for underwater travel. The inner hull protects the crew . But how does a submarine go down in a controlled way?

Like many ships, a submarine has ballast tanks. They are located between the inner and outer hulls. On the surface of the ocean, the sub's ballast tanks are filled with air. This makes the submarine less dense than the water. So it stays afloat. For the vessel to dive down, water is pumped into the ballast tanks. The added water makes the submarine denser and heavier. It starts to sink. At this point, the sub's "diving planes" are tilted down. These steel fins allow the craft to glide down.

Once underwater, the submarine can travel at different depths. How? Its diving planes can be tilted so that they lift the ship's nose or drop it down. Then the sub's propeller pushes the craft forward in that direction.

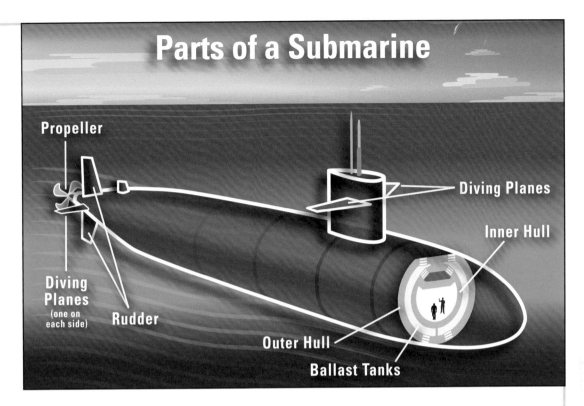

Parts of a Submarine

Propeller

Diving Planes

Inner Hull

Diving Planes (one on each side)

Rudder

Outer Hull

Ballast Tanks

Getting Back to the Surface

For the submarine to return to the surface, its ballast water must be pumped out. Air will replace it. This air is stored in containers, where it's packed very tightly. When released, the air blows the water from the tanks, then fills the tanks. Now the sub is less dense and starts to rise. Then, the diving planes lift the nose up, and the propeller pushes the sub to the surface.

Submarines are specially designed to travel both above and below the water's surface.

DID YOU KNOW ?

A Submarine's Special Rudder

Like other ships, a submarine uses its rudder for steering. But the submarine's rudder is shaped differently from the rudders on other ships. One part of the rudder stands above the outer hull. The other is below it.

Ships of the Future

If you could look ahead in time, you would probably see a new world of ships. Future vessels will likely be built with materials that need fewer repairs. They may be much bigger, too. That means they will have more space for cargo and people. Amazingly, a larger ship of tomorrow may have a smaller crew. Why? It will be more automated. In other words, the ship will do more work by itself.

Imagine such a ship. Its main computer plots out the best course to take. Once the ship leaves port, the computer keeps checking that everything runs smoothly. *Is the ship in the right position? Does the engine need to work harder? Is the rudder moving in the correct way? What are the stabilizers doing? Should the ship go faster?* Of course, the crew will still do work. But much of the crew's job will be watching over the computer and the ship's other machines.

Different but the Same

The ships of the future will likely be different from today's ships in many

ways. But one thing will stay the same. They will still be built to float in the water. Shipbuilders will still have to understand how buoyancy and density make all ships float.

This model shows what U.S. Navy destroyers may look like in the future.

DID YOU KNOW ?

Ancient Shipbuilders

People have been making simple boats for many thousands of years. About 6,000 years ago the ancient Egyptians began to make some major advances in shipbuilding. They made vessels that were long and narrow. People rowing with oars powered them. As time passed, the Egyptians added sails to their ships. The hulls were changed, too. They were built from long strips, or planks, of wood. This type of Egyptian ship became a model for builders around the world. In fact, thousands of years passed before iron hulls replaced wooden ones. Also, not until the 1800s did engines start replacing sails.

Glossary

amphibious—Able to function both in the water and on land.

ballast—Weight added to the **hull** to make it steady.

bow—The front of the **hull**.

bow thruster—A small **propeller** inside a cavity in the **hull**, near the **bow**.

bulkheads—Walls that divide a ship's **hull** into watertight areas called **compartments**.

buoyancy—The upward push of water on an object.

compartments—Closed-off areas on a **ship**; compartments are watertight areas.

density—The closeness of something's basic parts. The tighter an object's weight is packed, the greater is its density.

displace—To move from its place.

gravity—The force that pulls everything to Earth. This force gives everything weight.

helm—The ship's steering wheel. The helm controls the movement of the **rudder**.

hull—The ship's main body. The hull is watertight.

keel—A long, strong beam that runs along the entire base of the **hull** from the **bow** to the **stern**.

knot—The unit used by **ships** and other vessels to measure speed. One knot equals 1 nautical mile per hour. That equals 1.15 miles per hour (1.85 kilometers per hour).

navigator—A person who decides the course taken by a **ship** (or other craft).

ore—Rocks or minerals that have been mined and that have valuable metals in them.

pressure—A force, such as the force of water pushing against an object.

propeller—A group of blades attached to a center, called a hub. As the propeller turns, it moves the craft forward.

rudder—A movable flap on the back of a **ship** that is used to turn the **ship** to the left or right.

ship—A very large boat.

species—A group of animals or plants with basic things in common.

stabilizers—Fin-like surfaces found on each side of the **hull**. They keep the **ship** from rolling from side to side in rough water.

stern—The back of the **hull**. This area is the rear of the **ship**.

superstructure—All the structures on a ship above the main deck.

vessel—A large boat or a **ship**.

To Learn More

Read these books:

DK Publishing. *Submarine.* New York: Dorling Kindersley, 2003.

Kentley, Eric. *Boat.* New York: Dorling Kindersley, 2000.

Plisson, Phillip, and Anne Jankeliowitch. *Ships.* New York: Abrams Books for Young Readers, 2007.

Wilkinson, Philip. *The World of Ships.* Boston: Kingfisher, 2005.

Look up these Web sites:

Boat Safe Kids
http://www.boatsafe.com/kids/index.htm

Knots and Knotting (International Guild of Knot Tyers)
http://www.folsoms.net/knots

Songs of the Sea
http://www.contemplator.com/sea/index.html

Tall Ships Sailing Challenge
http://www.cbc.ca/kids/games/tallships

Water Science for Schools (U.S. Geological Survey)
http://ga.water.usgs.gov/edu/index.html

Key Internet search terms:

floating and sinking, ship, submarine, warship

Index

About the Author

Susan Markowitz Meredith likes to find out the how and why of things. She especially enjoys sharing what she discovers with young readers. So far, she has written more than 35 books on some very interesting topics. Meredith also has produced quite a few TV shows for young thinkers.